MY PET DIARY

FILL ME WITH THE

BE CREATIVE

LOVING WORDS

WONDERFUL MEMORIES

PHOTOS

ART

THIS CUTE BOOK

BELONGS TO

AND IT'S ALL ABOUT MY

PAWSOME

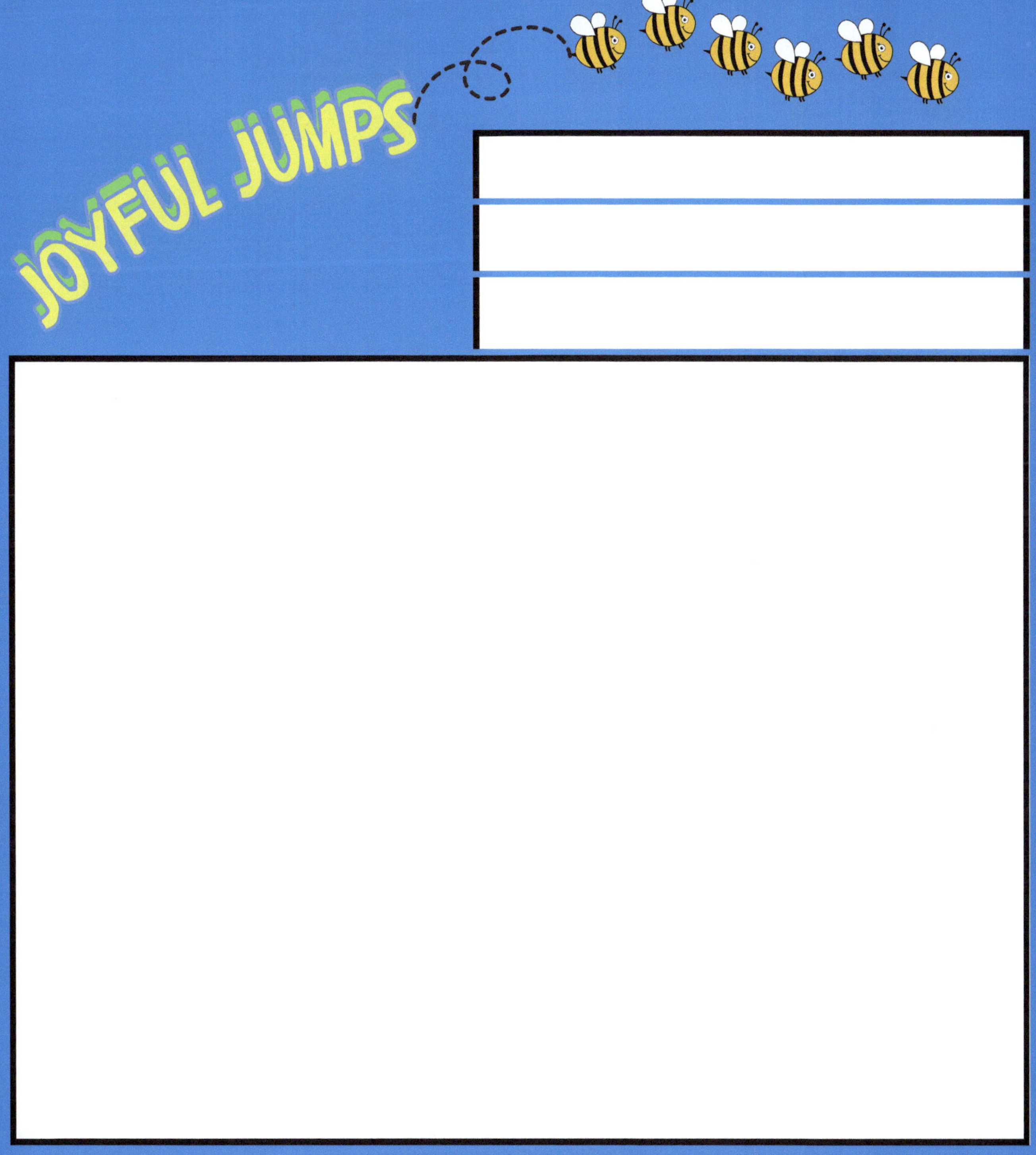

JOYFUL JUMPS

FUR-EVER

BARKTASTIC

CUTE

fluffy

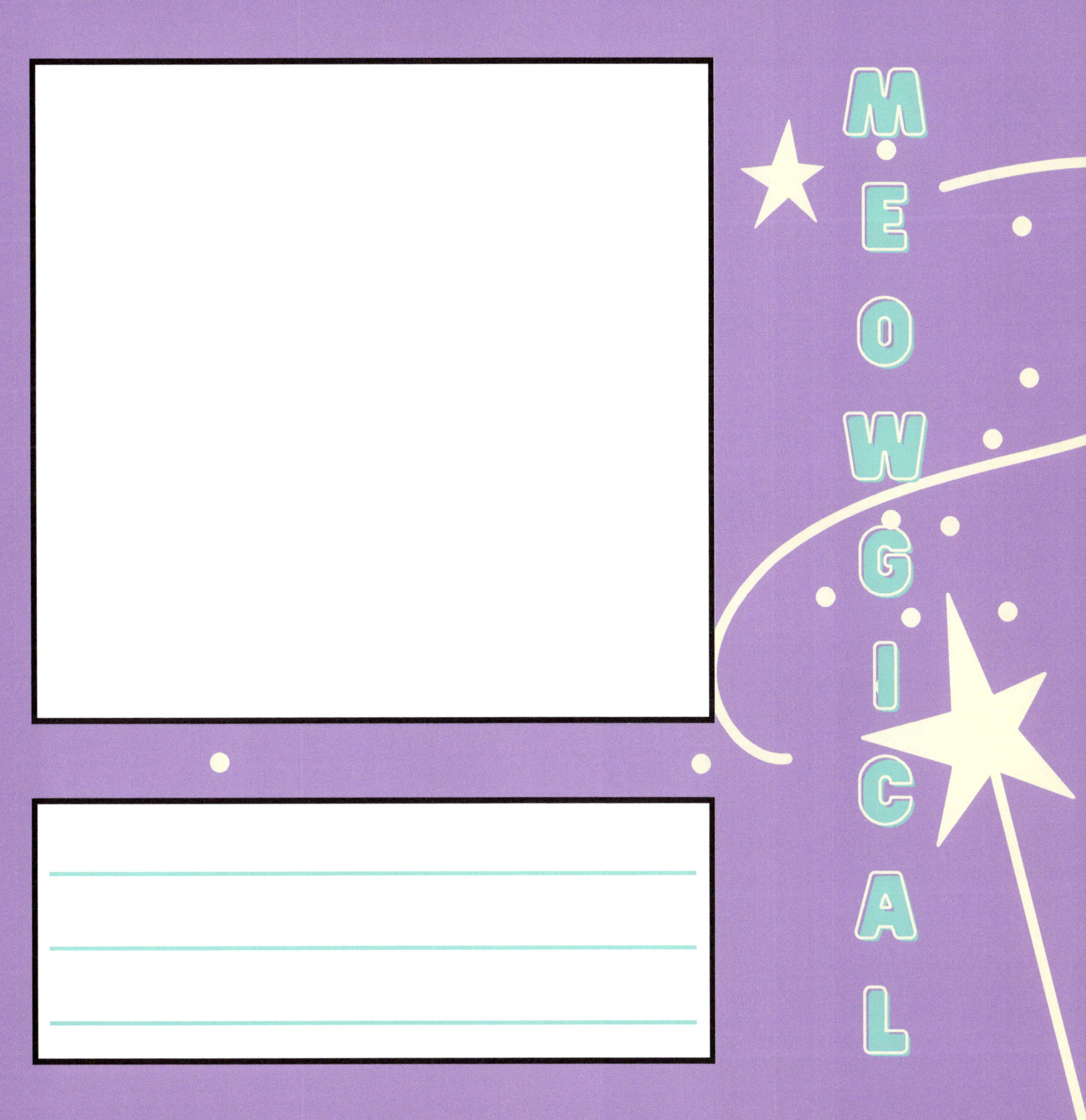

MEOWGICAL

CUDDLY

Pet-tastic

fuzzball

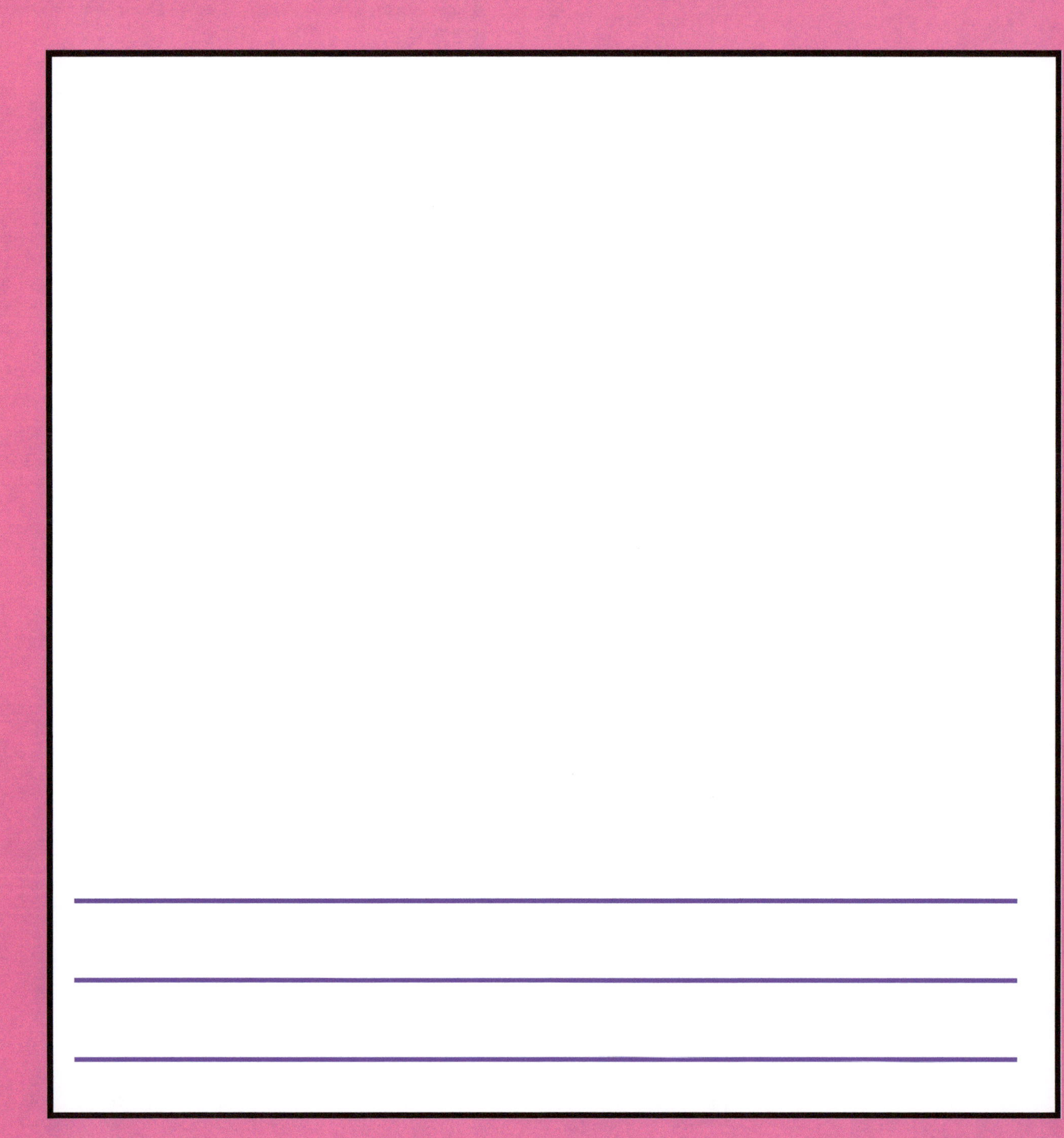

SQUEAK
HEART

BISCUIT BUDDIES

whisker wonders

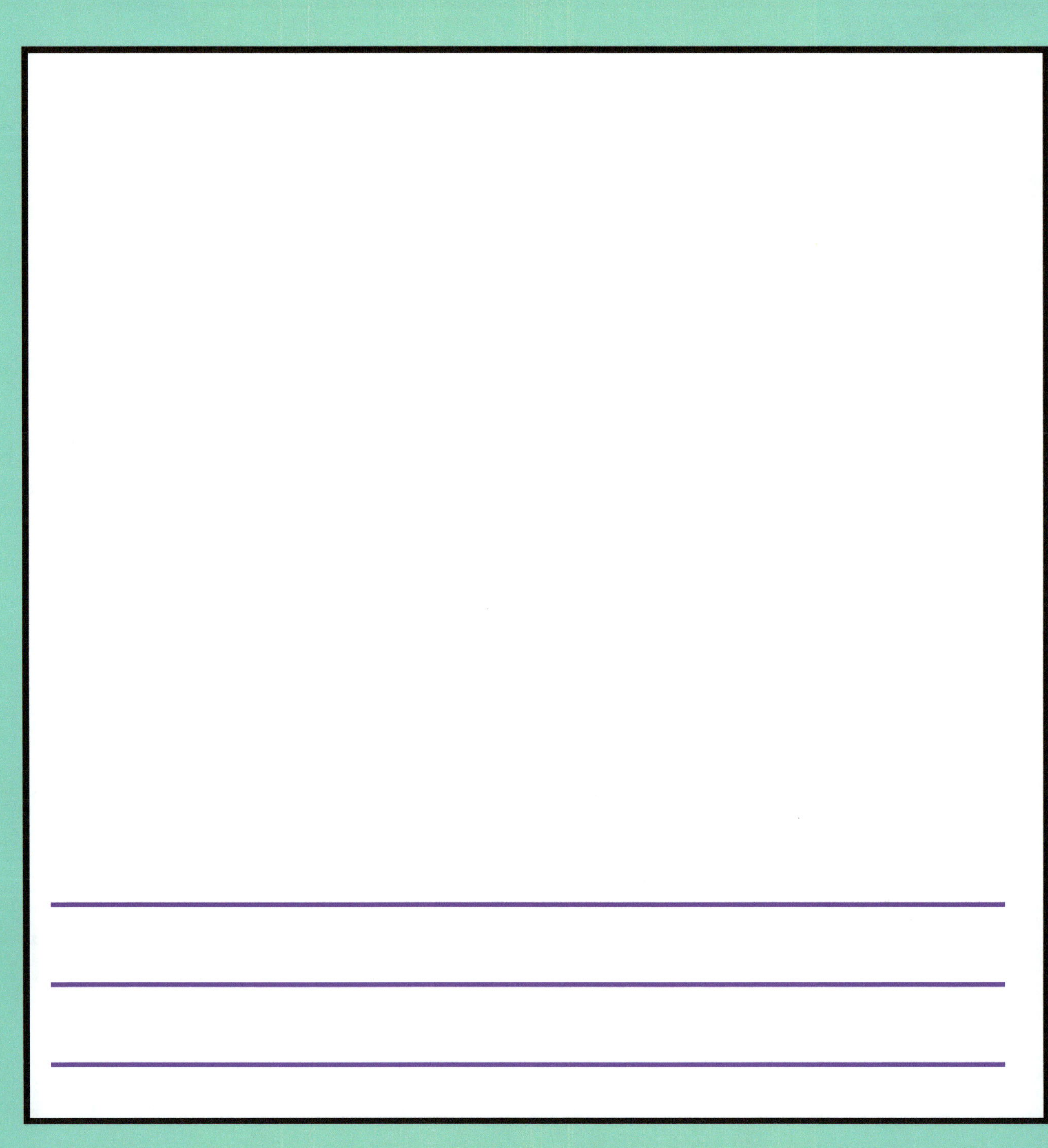

SNUGGLEBUG

belly rub bliss

FURENDSHIP

bestie

HAPPY TAILS

SNOUT
SMILES

ISBN 978-9918-9583-3-7